Table of Content

Introduction

Time slice under investigation (2000BC to 1000 BC) commences with the decline of the Indus Valley Civilization and the arrival of the Aryan tribes. The time slice ends with the departure of the Aryan tribes to the Ganga Jumna valleys. The period is one of great changes, a sophisticated civilization vanished and was replaced by relatively unsophisticated Indo European tribes, and this process however is one of great interest. The Aryans and their religion underwent two major changes, from pre Vedic Hinduism to Vedic Hinduism and subsequently to Classical Hinduism. The language also underwent a similar transformation to end up as Classical Sanskrit. The non Aryan language which we claim was proto Punjabi also evolved to Classical Punjabi. In this process the non Aryan population was enslaved and the Aryan tribes slowly gained ascendency. There was a two way exchange which resulted in the transformations in religion and language.

Unknown Neolithic populations lived in the region for millennia until sporadic settlements sprang up along the Indus Valley. These ancient settlements eventually culminated in the Indus Valley Civilization around 3000 B.C.E. The founders of this civilization are believed to be a Dravidian or Elamo-Dravidian people, but this remains difficult to verify, as there is no agreement on deciphering the Indus Valley script. The Indus Valley Civilization spanned much of what is today Pakistan and western India, but declined shortly prior to the rise of the Vedic Civilization which, according to the contested Aryan invasion theory, resulted from the arrival in the North of the Subcontinent of tribes from Central Asia. The two cultures mixed to produce the Vedic Civilization that existed between the Hakra-Ghakkar and Ganges rivers in what is now modern India around 1500 B.C.E. The Vedic Civilization helped shape subsequent cultures in South Asia.

This civilization, however, faded away by 1700 BCE, and was followed by a new stage in India's history. While it declined, India saw waves of migration from the mountainous northwest, by a people who referred to themselves as Aryans. The Aryans brought a distinctive language and way of life to the northern half of India and, after first migrating into the Punjab and Indus Valley, pushed east along the Ganges River and settled down into a life of farming and pastoralism.

As they interacted with indigenous peoples, a new period in India's history took shape. That period is known as the Vedic Age (1700 – 600 BCE).

During the long course of the Vedic Age, states formed in northern India. The surplus from farming and pastoralism allowed people to engage in a multitude of other occupations and made for a lively trade. Villages thus grew in number and some became towns. Consequently, there was a need for greater leadership, something that was provided by chieftains of the many Aryan clans. Over time, higher levels of political organization developed, and these chieftains became kings or the leaders of clan assemblies. By the end of the Vedic Age, northern India was divided up by sixteen major kingdoms and oligarchies.

Time Line

2000 BC: the civilization of the Indus Valley declines

2000 BC: the Kurgan culture spreads to Eastern Europe and northern Iran

1900 BC: Late Harappan Phase (Cemetery H Culture)

1700 BC: Indo-Iranians separate from the other Indo-European tribes and migrate eastward to settle in Iran

1700 BC: - The Iron Age begins in India.

1600 BC: Indo-Aryans invade India from the west and expel the Dravidians

1500 BC: religious texts are written in Vedic, an Indo-European language

1300 BC: Cemetery H culture comes to an end

1100 BC: the Indo-Aryans use iron tools

1000 BC: the Rig-Veda are composed

1000BC: Aryans migrate to the Ganga Jumna valleys

1000BC: Jatts arrive in the Punjab

The Indus Valley Civilization

. Indus Valley civilization (known also as Harappan culture) appeared around 2500 B.C. along the Indus River valley in Punjab and Sindh. This civilization, which had a writing system, urban centers, and a diversified social and economic system, was discovered in the 1920s at its two most important sites: Mohenjo-daro, in Sindh , and Harappa, in Punjab south of Lahore. A number of other lesser sites stretching from the Himalayan foothills in Indian Punjab to Gujarat east of the Indus River and to Balochistan to the west have also been discovered and studied. How closely these places were connected to Mohenjo-daro and Harappa is not clearly known, but evidence indicates that there was some link and that the people inhabiting these places were probably related.

The major sites of this civilization are in Pakistan. In fact it is in Pakistan that an earlier phase of it has also been unearthed. Between 1955to 1957, a Pakistani archaeologist, F.A.Khan, discovered a town of the pre-Indus period (c. 3300-2800 B.C), at Kot Diji in Khairpur, Sind. Such sites were also discovered by Rafique Mughal in Bahawalpur, especially in the Cholistan desert, extending the area of this culture to the whole of southern Pakistan. The area was further extended by Professor Ahmad Hasan Dani, the famous Pakistani archaeologist and Sanskritologist, when he discovered the sites of this civilization at Gumla, seven miles from Dera Ismail Khan. In fact Dani identified six cultural periods and Professor Farzand Ali Durrani , who excavated Rahman Dheri which is fourteen miles north of Dera Ismail Khan city, provided more details about the extension of this civilization in the North West Frontier Province.

The Indus Valley civilization primarily comprised of the people who migrated much before the Aryans from South East Europe. The Dravidian language has been found akin to the ancient Turanians or Scythanians language. The Vedic Aryans described them as "flat-nosed "or "nose less' monsters and described as a 'godless black-faced tribe", without rites or sacrifice, they are described as living in cites and well-built dwellings.

The Hindu god Indria described as "destroying the cities of the Asuras and humiliating their defenders,', "destroying the cities of the Dasyus ; and : :demolishing the hostile and ungodly cities". Agni is likewise said to have celebrated as "having destroyed the spacious iron walled cities of the Dasyus" and having slain them. It is not clear at all what is being referred to here, the IVC cities had in all probability been abandoned or almost abandoned by the time the Aryans arrived, the cites with a few exceptions were not heavily fortified , the people were not possibly flat nosed black faced. It would seem that there is some poetic license and the fact that the account was written by Aryans, and is therefore exaggerated and not much can be inferred from this.

The IVC population differed entirely from the Vedic Aryans, in IVC there was no caste system (although it need to be said that at the time of arrival the Vedic Aryans also did not practice caste system), the dead were buried, the widows of the IVC people remarry in fact usually remarry the younger brother of the deceased, curiously a custom which Jats practiced.

Archaeologists disagree whether the Kot -Diji type of cultural artifacts constitute a separate civilization or an early phase of the same civilization. Rafique Mughal, citing evidence from the excavations at Bahawalpur and Cholistan, concluded that 'all Kot Diji-related sites *together* constitute an Early Harappan or early urban, formative phase of the Indus Civilization'. However, Parpola argues that the term is misleading because it 'suggests discontinuity, like pre-Aryan vs. Aryan'. In fact, many scholars treat the latter culture as a changed form of the earlier one. This is significant because, if the dates of the Indus Valley Culture are approximately 2300-2000 B.C, and the dates of the kot Diji one are c. 3300-2800, then the length of the period of urban civilization in South Asia have been pushed back a thousand years.

The area of the early culture is given by Mughal as follows: . The central-northern areas of Baluchistan, the greater portion of Sind and the Punjab, Kalibangan on the Indian side, and the south-western part of the Frontier Province are the regions which are likely to have been comprised within the limits of the Kot Dijian culture. Indus Valley civilization was essentially a city culture sustained by surplus agricultural produce and extensive commerce, which included trade with Sumer in southern Mesopotamia in what, is today modern Iraq.

Copper and bronze were in use, but not iron. Mohenjo-Daro and Harappa were cities built on similar plans of well-laid-out streets, elaborate drainage systems, public baths, differentiated residential areas, flat-roofed brick houses and fortified administrative and religious centers enclosing meeting halls and granaries. Weights and measures were standardized. Distinctive engraved stamp seals were used, perhaps to identify property. Cotton was spun, woven, and dyed for clothing. Wheat, rice, and other food crops were cultivated, and a variety of animals were domesticated. Wheel-made pottery -- some of it adorned with animal and geometric motifs -- has been found in profusion at all the major Indus sites. A centralized administration has been inferred from the cultural uniformity revealed, but it remains uncertain whether authority lay with a priestly or a commercial oligarchy.

By far the most exquisite but most obscure artifacts unearthed to date is the small, square steatite seals engraved with human or animal motifs. Large numbers of the seals have been found at Mohenjo-Daro, many bearing pictographic inscriptions generally thought to be a kind of script.

The IVC by 2000 BC was in decline. But all the regions including in the northeast and south east, continued to be loosely linked to the core Indus Civilization for hundreds of years after this.

The central authority .which had for long, enforced homogeneity over the vast area, collapsed. In addition, there were new arrivals as well. Many Harrapan artifacts' like: stamp seals; triangular cakes; miniature carts frame and wheels; perforated pottery; cubical weights; fixed sized brick; and script characters, all disappeared. Several settlements were abandoned; smaller settlements instead were established, external trade came to an end

The Indus Valley Civilization has no successor, the later smaller urban settlements did not have the detail and precision in town planning, fired bricks appear only rarely, figures of animals and deities on seals and tablets became exceedingly rare. The terracotta figurines, especially of the Mother Goddess, are not to be found, there was a major change in burial practices, suggesting radical changes in the religion. The Indus weights are no longer used, the Indus pottery is replaced by other, generally coarser, forms.

The High degree of homogeneity shown in the mature stage, 2500 BC to 2000 BC began to show signs of breaking up. In excavations in uppermost layers, the standards of the construction of buildings had deteriorated and the artifacts recovered from these layers were of lower quality .The progressive deviations from the standards continued till about 1700 BC but the linkage of the outlying regions remained intact. After 1700 BC this linkage began to weaken and the civilization split into three parts.

During the late pr post mature Harrapan phase the Upper Indus Valley had apparently no or very weak links with the lower Indus Valley regions. The Arabian sea coastal areas   and the hinterlands represented by the assemblage of Kulli, Jhukar, Surkotada, Rangpir etc. were linked initially to constitute a long coastal belt having common interests to carry trade or exchange by sea until a long period after the demise of the IVC civilization

The northern region comprised the northern Indus plains, and the Hakra –Ghakkar Valley. Harrapa became the center of the central part. . Mohenjadaro was the main city of the eastern part which comprised lower Indus valley and eastern Baluchistan The demise of IVC followed with a period where cities disappear , settlement sizes are small , less than 40 hectares.

Cemetery H Culture:

The late Harrapan phase in Sindh, is known as, the phase, represented by sites like Junkar, Amri, Chanhubaro. In Gujarat the late phase is known as the Rangpur phase comprising of Rangpur, Lothal, and Rojdi. The late Harrapan phase in Punjab is called as Cemetery H phase. The Jhukar culture is named after a site little north of Mohenjodaro , the pottery is of a different design , seals become circular

The cultures that followed were small scale and rural, without city life and writing, using fewer raw materials that originated elsewhere at great distances. The long distance trade diminished and was restricted to the Eastern and South Eastern e parts only which were no longer firmly tied to the whole civilization. Few of these residual cultures produced metals in any great quantity, and few metal tools were found.

The **Cemetery H culture** was a Bronze Age culture in the Punjab region in the northern part of the Indian subcontinent, from about 1900 BCE until about 1300 BCE. It was a regional form of the late phase of the Harappan (Indus Valley) civilization (alongside the Jhukar culture of Sindh and Rangpur culture of Gujarat). .The Jhunkar culture was inferior to the Harrapan Civilization. There was no writing; there are fewer sites all located in the Sindh. It is a non-urban culture, characterized by "crude handmade pottery" and "campsites of a population which was nomadic and mainly pastoralist

The Cemetery H culture was located in and around the Punjab region in present-day India and Pakistan. It was named after a cemetery found in "area H" at Harappa. Remains of the culture have been dated from about 1900 BCE until about 1300 BCE. Bricks used were of smaller size, but the construction was poor, the pottery was of a completely different design, burial practices also changed , a large pottery urns were used to bury the body

According to Rafique Mughal, the Cemetery H culture developed out of the northern part of the Indus Valley Civilization around 1700 BCE, being part of the Punjab Phase, one of three cultural phases that developed in the Localization Era or "Late Harappan phase" of the Indus Valley Tradition. According to Kenoyer, the Cemetery H culture "may only reflect a change in the focus of settlement organization from that which was the pattern of the earlier Harappan phase and not cultural discontinuity, urban decay, invading aliens, or site abandonment, all of which have been suggested in the past."

According to Kennedy and Mallory & Adams, the Cemetery H culture also "shows clear biological affinities" with the earlier population of Harappa Some traits of the Cemetery H culture have been associated with the Swat culture, which has been regarded as evidence of the Indo-Aryan movement toward the Indian subcontinent.

According to Parpola, the Cemetery H culture represents a first wave of Indo-Aryan migration from as early as 1900 BCE, which was followed by a migration to the Punjab c. 1700-1400 BCE. According to Kochhar, the Swat IV co-founded the Harappan Cemetery H phase in Punjab (2000-1800 BCE), while the Rigvedic Indo-Aryans of Swat V later absorbed the Cemetery H people and gave rise to the Painted Grey Ware culture (to 1400 BCE).

Together with the Gandhara grave culture. The distinguishing features of this culture include:

- The use of cremation of human remains. The bones were stored in painted pottery burial urns. This is completely different from the Indus civilization where bodies were buried in wooden coffins. The urn burials and the "grave skeletons" were nearly contemporaneous.
- Reddish pottery, painted in black with antelopes, peacocks etc., sun or star motifs, with different surface treatments to the earlier period.
- Expansion of settlements into the east.
- Rice became a main crop.
- Apparent breakdown of the widespread trade of the Indus civilization, with materials such as marine shells no longer used.
- Continued use of mud brick for building.
-

The question that what happened to the people of IVC has troubled historians. My opinion is that a significant part of the Hindus Dalit, Untouchables population is in fact the descendents of the people of IVC and these were enslaved and moved with the Arya to the Ganga Jumna Valleys.

A portion of the IVC population emigrated to the South and a smaller portion stayed back. Just after the Arya moved to the Ganga Jumna valleys the Jutts ot Jats or Jutes moved from their abode in South East Europe to Punjab and soon became rulers. They enjoyed ascendency for a long period of time until the Alexander invasion which dented their hold on the Pakistani Punjab. But this is beyond the period of investigations of this book and therefore is left lest we digress.

Impact of Indus Valley Civilization on Religious thought after the demise of IVC

The Indus Valley Civilization after its demise was partially and incompletely replicated by a number of cultures which persisted for a periods. The physical infrastructure tradition and techniques also did not persist at least not in its entirety. What did persist was the belief system, , the system upon which the civilization was built, the subsequent Jainism, Buddhism , Bakti and Sikhism religions and or movements suggest that these non Vedic movements were most likely evolved from the belief system of the dead civilization. Much later in Punjab's history the same belief system encouraged and facilitated the introduction of the Sufic movement.

Sacred Hindu scriptures Vedas were composed here. Panini defined the grammar of Sanskrit on this land and Patanjali wrote Yoga Sutras in Punjab. The descendants of most of the Hindu Gods, that all of India worships are the Khatris of Punjab, the only true Kshatriyas. Jainism and Nath traditions have roots in Punjab. Buddhism flourished here in Taxila, and a secular Sufism challenged the fascist Sharia in Punjab.

Jainism and Buddhism emerged as the most potent religious reform movements during later Vedic period. Both Jainism and Buddhism were founded in the 6th century BC, and they sprung out of the same roots. Buddhism and Jainism are two ancient religions that developed in Magadha (Bihar) and continue to thrive in the modern age. Mahavira and Gautama Buddha are generally accepted as contemporaries.

Jainism originated in the 7th–5th century BCE in the Ganges basin of eastern India, the scene of intense religious speculation and activity at that time. Buddhism also appeared in this region, as did other belief systems that renounced the world and opposed the ritualistic Brahmanic schools whose prestige derived from their claim of purity and their ability to perform the traditional rituals and sacrifices and to interpret their meaning. These new religious perspectives promoted asceticism, the abandonment of ritual, domestic and social action, and the attainment of spiritual illumination in an attempt to win, through one's own efforts, freedom from repeated rebirth (samsara).

The *Sramanas* movement, which originated in the culture of world renunciation that emerged in India from about the 7th century BCE, was the common origin of many religious and philosophical traditions in India, including the Charvaka school, Buddhism, and its sister religion, Jainism. The *Sramanas* were renunciants who rejected the Vedic teachings, which was the traditional religious order in India, and renounced conventional society.

Jainism and Buddhism share many features, terminology and ethical principles, but emphasize them differently. Both are śramaṇa ascetic traditions that believe it is possible to attain liberation from the cycle of rebirths and deaths (samsara) through spiritual and ethical disciplines They differ in some core doctrines such as those on asceticism, Middle Way versus *Anekantavada*, and self versus no-self (*jiva, atta, anatta*) In Buddha's time a reorientation of faith was possibly warranted by the impact of Indus Valley Civilization belief system. Yogic meditations, ascetic habits and belief in transmigration may have come from non Aryan sources.

Jainism seems to be older than Buddhism, Mahavira who lived from 599 BC to 527 BC was not the founder of the religion, his predecessor Parvsa who lived 250 years ago was also a historical figure. The ahisma doctrine preached by Rsabha is possibly prior in time to the advent of the Aryans in India . Ahimsa is the chief religious idea; it does not mean merely a negative virtue of non-violence but also is based on the positive quality of universal love which is the result of recognition of kinship amongst all living things. In Jain thought even gods cannot directly achieve liberation; they must be born as human beings before they can   hope to get salvation. The human soul by its practice of penance is able to climb up different stages , step by step, becomes purer and purer at every stage till it reaches spiritual glory and perfection , from where there is no going back.

The **Bhakti movement** refers to the theistic devotional trend that emerged in medieval Hinduism and later acted as the de facto catalyst to the formation and subsequent revolutionized in the form of Sikhism. It originated in eighth-century south India (now Tamil Nadu and Kerala), and spread northwards. The Bhakti movement empowered those on the lowest rungs of Indian society. The rigid caste system, the complicated ritualism that constituted the practice of worship and the inherent need to move to a more fulfilling method of worship and salvation perhaps spurred this movement.

Bhakti poets emphasized surrender to god. Equally, many of the Bhakti saints were rebels who chose to defy the currents of their time through their writings. The Bhakti tradition continues in a modified version even in the present day. Kabir preached a monotheism that appealed directly to the poor and assured them of their access to god without an intermediary. He rejected both Hinduism and Islam, as well as empty religious rituals, and denounced hypocrisy. This outraged the orthodox gentry .But Kabir was not to be cowed down. He was something of a lone wolf, not afraid to stand up for himself and his beliefs.

Another singer-songwriter was **Guru Nanak** (1469-1539), an iconoclast and, yes, critic of the dominant societal values of his time. Nanak was of a syncretic mindset and attempted to fuse the tenets of Hinduism and Islam to serve as a guide for all humanity. He rebelled against a society that preferred ritual to devotion and sincerity. Among the institutions that he challenged was caste. Nanak did not subscribe to caste taboos and was contemptuous of its ideas of "high" and "low". Given the injunctions against intermingling, Nanak frequently travelled with **Mardana**, a lower-caste Mirasi (a community of dancers and singers). Mardana was a skilled rubab player who is said to have accompanied Nanak whenever he sang his verses. Eventually, Nanak founded a separate religion**, Sikhism**, which attempted to put his precepts into practice. Inspite of mention of various names of gods and goddesses the Sikhs remained opposed to polytheistisc ideas. God is envisaged by Guru Nanak as sole creator of all that is visible or invisible

A near-contemporary of Nanak was **Ravi Dass** (1450-1520), who was born into a family of leather workers (chamars) in Varanasi. Like Nanak, Ravi Dass too spoke of the need for a casteless society, though, unlike Nanak, he had suffered its slings and arrows as he belonged to an untouchable caste. In one of his popular poems, Ravi Dass speaks of "Begumpura"—"a place with no pain, no taxes or cares... no wrongdoing, worry, terror or torture" (translated by Hawley and Juergensmeyer in Songs of the Saints of India). In this verse and in many others, Ravi Dass gave voice to lower-caste pain at Brahminical society's treatment of them. The Ravidassia community that continues to flourish to this day is evidence of the everlasting nature of his appeal.

While Kabir, Ravi Dass and Nanak spoke of the formless god (nirgun bhakti), **Meerabai** (1498-1546) from Rajasthan composed and sung devotional verses in praise of Krishna. Meera's intense devotion to Krishna in defiance of patriarchal norms was a rebellious act. Her determination to be united with the lord she thought of as her beloved was a source of deep friction within her family, but Meera held steady nevertheless.

The Bhakti movement empowered the underbelly of Indian society in fundamental ways and also provided the required impetus for the growth of vernacular literature. This tradition of those deemed "low" singing and writing did not, however, end with the Bhakti movement comingling into the mainstream. In 19th century Karnataka, **Shishunala Sharif** (1819-89) was an influential figure. A Muslim by birth, Sharif also accepted the tenets of Hinduism and often sang of communal harmony.

During the freedom struggle, the poet-revolutionary Ram Prasad "Bismil" (1897-1927) composed the songs "Sarfaroshi ki tamanna ab hamare dil mein hai and Rang de basanti chola" that were sung by many revolutionaries.

Sufism has played a major role in the history of Punjab. West Punjab is heavily influenced by Sufi Saints and major Sufi Pirs. The partition in 1947 led to the almost complete departure of Muslims from East Punjab. ... After the partition the Dalit community took over the care of Sufi shrines in the East Punjab. Sufism known as Tasawwuf in the Arabic-speaking world is a form of Islamic mysticism that emphasizes introspection and spiritual closeness with the God. It is a mystical form of Islam, a school of practice that emphasizes the inward search for The God and shuns materialism. "Sufism is a religion of intense devotion; Love is its manifestation, poetry, music and dance are the instruments of its worship and attaining oneness with God is its ideal." In other words, it implies that the ideal before an individual should be to be one with God. For the attainment of this ideal, intense devotion for God is needed in the individual. Devotion is reflected in love. This love for the Almighty is expressed through three fold activities on the part of the individual i.e. poetry of love towards God, music of love towards God and dance of love towards God.

Ishtiaq Ahmed writes: The Sufi brotherhoods that arrived in South Asia from the Middle East and central Asia had already been influenced by the pantheistic traditions of South Asia, and in some cases the result was theist fusions or unitarian views of God. It is, however, important to point out that some Sufi orders were quite conservative such as the Suhrawardia and Naqshbandia. They had a strong presence in the Punjab. The Naqshbandi Sufi, Ahmed Sirhindi or Mujadid Alf-Sani, who lived during the 16th century and is buried at Sirhind in the Indian East Punjab, played an important role in the revival of strict Islam in the Mughal Empire and indeed in the Punjab.

On the other hand, non-conformist philosophical and theosophical ideas and movements emanating from Islamic and Hindu roots gave birth to interesting syntheses and syncretism. Some individual Sufis evolved radical non-conformist positions that decried the dogmatic forms of religion, whether Islam or Hinduism. The basic idea that gained acceptance in such circles was that ultimately there is one Great Spirit or God holding together the cosmic and earthly systems. Therefore, they conceived humanity as one great family with its different manifestations in terms of religions and cultures.

In practical and symbolic terms this is illustrated rather well from the 16th century by the close friendship between the Sufi poet, Hussain of Lahore (b. 1538), and the Hindu Brahmin youth, Madho Lal, from the nearby village of Shahdara. To this day an annual festival, the Madho-Lal Hussain Mela, is held on the outskirts of Lahore to commemorate their union. They are buried in the same tomb, to which thousands of people flock on this ceremonial occasion.

Hussain broke away from orthodoxy. He danced and drank wine and lived a life of defiance. The Mughal Emperor Akbar was in power at Agra at that time and he too weakened the hold of dogmatism. Therefore this was a period of Hindu-Muslim symbiosis both at the level of the Mughal state -- of which the Punjab was one possession -- and among the common people.

Sultan Bahu (born 1639) was another Sufi who continued to question the compatibility of orthodox and the non--conformist worldview of radical Sufism. He was a prolific writer, whose message displayed the inevitable tension between a rigid worldview dichotomising social reality into Islamic and non-Islamic categories.

Such a train of thinking reached its apogee under Bulleh Shah (1680-1758). Bulleh Shah's murshid or spiritual master, Shah Inayat, belonged to the Qadriyya Shattari School: known for its close affinity with yoga and other meditative practices.

One day some rich but God-fearing man had deposited a great deal of wealth with Shah Inayat with the supplication that he should distribute it among needy people. Shah Inayat told Bulleh Shah, 'Distribute this wealth among the poor and needy in accordance with the law of God'.

A crowd of needy people had gathered at the spot in the hope of getting something. Bulleh Shah told one of them to take everything and to the rest he gave nothing. Such a decision caused a stir and people began to complain and agitate. Shah Inayat too was perplexed by this decision.

He asked Bulleh Shah admonishingly to explain what he had done. Bulleh Shah said, 'You told me to distribute the wealth according to the law of God. I did exactly that. Just look around. There are a few rich people and the vast majority are poor and dispossessed. So, I followed the divine law which works in this world'.

Shah Inayat Qadri could not deny the force of the argument put forward by his disciple. Thus began a long association between the two but the disciple developed even more radical non-conformist views. Some of Bulleh Shah's verses are worth quoting:

Masjid dha de, mandir dha de, dha de jo kucch dainda

Par kisi da dil na dhain, Rab dilan vich rehnda

Tear down the Mosque, tear down the temple

Tear down every thing in sight

But don't (tear down) break anyone's heart

Because God lives there

Then he writes:

Gal samajh laee te raolaa keeh

eyh Raam, Raheem te Maulaa keeh?

Why all this commotion if you claim understanding?

Why this fuss about calling Him Ram, Rahim or Moula?

(Ram is a Hindu god; Rahim and Moula are Allah's designations)

About priests in general Bulleh Shah writes:

Mulla tay mashaalchi dohaan ikko chit

Loukan karday chananan, aap anhairae vich

Mullah and the torch-bearer, both from the same flock

Guiding others; themselves in the dark

The rebel Sufis were cosmopolitans. They lived simple lives and shunned the company of the rich and powerful. The ruling elite therefore always looked upon them with suspicion and perhaps even fear. However, such Sufis remained rebels in intellectual terms. They were not social revolutionaries.

The enlightened and composite tradition of the Punjab remained firm and steadfast well into the 19th and 20th centuries, when power had passed into the hands of the British. Mian Muhammad (1830-1904) and Khawaja Ghulam Farid (1841-1901) continued to preach universal peace and brotherhood. Many Hindus and Sikhs were disciples of Muslim Sufis.

In January 2005 I met a Hindu gentleman at Patiala, Amrik Chand Ahluwalia – 80 years of age -- who told me his family was disciples of a Muslim Sufi whose shrine was located on the border of Punjab and Balochistan. As a child his family and he had travelled to that place to perform ziarat. He told me that his family ate meat (goat and chicken) but only if it was slaughtered according to Islamic ritual. Some Muslims had continued to live in Patiala despite the exodus of 1947, and more from the neighbouring states of Haryana and UP had settled in Patiala afterwards and now getting halal meat was no problem.

This revelation was quite interesting. I pondered if a comparable Muslim adherence to Hindu values can be discerned in our Muslim Punjabi environment. It occurred to me that in our West Punjab homes eating beef was never popular and even now nobody relishes eating beef or serving it to guests.

So a fusion of Hindu and Islamic beliefs and practices has survived into the current period despite nearly 60 years of the partition of the Punjab. For this we must thank the syncretism of the rebel Sufis of the Punjab. :

There is evidence of reference to the Mother Goddess in Punjabi Sufi poetry.

Shah Hussian:

Oh my mother, who shall I tell

The Pain that I feel on account of separation from by beloved

Afzal Ahsan Ranhhawa:

I used to swim the mighty river

I am now paddling in tiny waters –oh mother

I have so many gashes in my body

As the number of hairs on your head, oh mother

Henceforth do not suckle the new born

Let him starve and die oh mother

The above could be reference to the Mother Goddesses, if indeed these are such reference it would imply that the IVC beliefs survived in the Punjab in some form or other, there have to be schools of learning or centers of philosophical thought, or perhaps these were oral traditions preserved orally. Popular sufi renderings like Shahbaz Qalande was sung (Many Bahanj like " Lal mare rakho jullaye lalan" not much old but its one version comes without " Sakhi shabahz Qalandar") without reference to Shahbaz Qalander in earlier days , similarly some folk stories of the Punjab were altered and in the original form could well be the lost inputs from the IVC. Possibly Granath has some more ancient Punjab couplets which were reused by Gurus, only they have reference from they found these, these references are not available. There is legend of "Punja Phollah Rani" the legend, has possible origin in Harrapan times. Heer Ranja and other love strues of the Punjab possibly have roots in older stories, which could have roots to the ancient civilization.

Dabistan-I Magahib mentions that when Kabir was in search of spiritual guide he visited the best of sufi Musalman and Hindus . The expression of Kabirs teachings was shaped by that of sufi saints and peots. Kabir speaks about cup of love of the lover (ashiq and habib) aiul the beloved (washua mahbub } of the path and its statious (muaam) etc. which were derived from Sufism '

Like Kabir Nanak is said to have had long discussions with Shaikh Sharaf of Panipat, the Pirs of Multan and Shaikh Ibrahlir., the successor of Shaikh farid at pakpattan. Undoubtly Nanak enjoyed the company of Sufi saints . We also find an evidence regarding   meeting with Shaikh Abdul Quddus Oangohi and was greatly influenced by the teachings of the Shaikh. It is also said that Nanak also came in contact with Shaikh Koharamad   (of Owalior) Guru Nanak travelled to Baghdad to visit the famous Qadiri centre of   shaikh Abdul Qadir Jilani Like Bhakti saints sufi saints also seem to have an urgent desire to meet the Bhaktas, were affected by each other. Shaikh Abdur Aahman Chlshti Combined both the bairaai and Mmiahid tradition about Kabir .

Centers of learning in the Punjab

Multan is one of the oldest cities in South Asia, though its exact age has yet to be determined. It has seen a lot of warfare because of its location on a major invasion route between South and Central Asia. It is famous for its Sufi shrines. Ancient name of Multan was Kashep Puri. The town was built by Raja Kashep After Hurnakas his son Parhilaad succeeded the throne and the town was then named after him as Parhilaad Puri. The current name Multan was given due to Mali people who were defeated by Alexander the Great. Once Keshap Puri (Multan) was capital of the Raja Hurnakas where Persian Kings had built temple of sun in which idol of sun was laid. After the conquest of Multan one Brahman had poined out Muhammad bin Qasim about treasure hidden beneath the fountain which was buried by Raja Jesubin. Muhammad bin Qasim found 330 chests of treare containing 13300 maunds gold. Entire treasure was shifted from Debal to Basra on ships. The most important place of the Hindu period was the "Surya Mandir". It was named after Sun god **Aditiya**, which is was shortened to Band even **Ayt** as in the case of **Aditwara** (or Aytwar) for Sunday. The ruins of Sun Mandir are located near the High Court of Multan.

A legend based on oral traditions holds that **Lahore**, known in ancient times as *Lavapuri* (City of Lava in Sanskrit), was founded by Prince Lava, the son of Sita and Rama; Kasur was founded by his twin brother Prince Kusha. To this day, Lahore Fort has a vacant Lava temple dedicated to Lava hence *Loh-awar* or "The Fort of Loh"). Some historians trace the history of the city as far back as 4000 years ago. However, historically, it has been proved that Lahore is at least 2,000 years old. Lying on the main trade and invasion routes to South Asia, Lahore has been ruled and plundered by a number of dynasties and hordes. Little is known of the history of the settlement prior to the Muslim period. The city of "Labokla" mentioned in Ptolemy's 2nd-century *Guide to Geography* may have been Lahore. No definitive records exist to elucidate Lahore's earliest history, and Lahore's ambiguous early histories have given rise to various theories about its establishment and history. Hindu legend states that Keneksen, the founder of the Great Suryavansha dynasty, is believed to have migrated out from the city

Ancient **Taxila** was an important city of Ancient India, situated at the pivotal junction of the Indian subcontinent and Central Asia. The origin of Taxila as a city goes back to c. 1000 BCE. By some accounts, the University of Ancient Taxila was considered to be one of the earliest universities in the world. In Vedic texts such as the Shatapatha Brahmana, it is mentioned that the Vedic philosopher Uddalaka Aruni (c. 7th century BCE) had travelled to the region of Gandhara. In later Buddhist texts, the Jatakas, it is specified that Taxila was the city where Aruni and his son Shvetaketu each had received their education. One of the earliest mentions of Taxila is in Pāṇini's *Aṣṭādhyāyī*, a Sanskrit grammar treatise dated to the 5th century BCE. Ahmad Hasan Dani and Saifur Rahman Dar trace the etymology of Taxila to a tribe called the Takka.

Takshila became a melting pot of cultures as students converged there from far lands. It is said that many influential Indian scholars composed their epoch-making work while teaching at Takshila. It is believed that Chanakya wrote Arthashastra – an ancient Indian treatise on economic policy and military strategy – during his teaching tenure at Takshila University. Maharishi Charak also composed his medical treatise Charak Samhita at Takshila university. The revered Sanskrit scholar and grammarian Panini also taught at Takshila. It's at Takshila where he produced his best work called Ashtadhyayi (eight chapters) – a complex, rule-based grammar book of Sanskrit that survives in its entirety to this day.

Much of the Hindu epic, the Mahabharata, is a conversation between Vaishampayana (a pupil of the sage, Vyasa) and King Janamejaya. It is traditionally believed that the story was first recited by Vaishampayana at the behest of Vyasa during the snake sacrifice performed by Janamejaya at Takshashila. The audience also included Ugrashravas, an itinerant bard, who would later recite the story to a group of priests at an ashram in the Naimisha Forest from where the story was further disseminated. The Kuru Kingdom's heir, Parikshit (grandson of Arjuna) is said to have been enthroned at Takshashila.

The Ramayana describes Takshashila as a magnificent city famed for its wealth which was founded by Bharata, the younger brother of Rama. Bharata, who also founded nearby Pushkalavati, installed his two sons, Taksha and Pushkala, as the rulers of the two cities.

In the Buddhist Jatakas, Taxila is described as the capital of the kingdom of Gandhara and a great centre of learning with world-famous teachers. The Takkasila Jataka, more commonly known as the Telapatta Jataka, tells the tale of a prince of Benares who is told that he would become the king of Takkasila if he could reach the city within seven days without falling prey to the yakkhinis who waylaid travellers in the forest. According to the Dipavamsa, one of Taxila's early kings was a Kshatriya named Dipankara who was succeeded by twelve sons and grandsons. *Kuñjakarṇa*, mentioned in the Avadanakalpalata, is another king associated with the city.

In the Jain tradition, it is said that Rishabha, the first of the Tirthankaras, visited Taxila millions of years ago. His footprints were subsequently consecrated by Bahubali who erected a throne and a dharmachakra ("wheel of the law") over them several miles in height and circumference.

The region around Taxila was settled by the neolithic era,   some ruins at Taxila dating to 3360 BCE. Ruins dating from the Early Harappan period around 2900 BCE have also been discovered in the Taxila area,though the area was eventually abandoned after the collapse of the Indus Valley Civilisation.

The first major settlement at Taxila, in Hathial mound, was established around 1000 BCE. By 900 BCE, the city was already involved in regional commerce, as discovered pottery shards reveal trading ties between the city and Puṣkalāvatī Taxila became a noted centre of learning (including the religious teachings of Buddhism) at least several centuries BCE, and continued to attract students from around the old world until the destruction of the city in the 5th century. It has been suggested that at its height, Taxila exerted a sort of "intellectual suzerainty" over other centres of learning in India and its primary concern was not with elementary, but higher education. Generally, a student entered Taxila at the age of sixteen. The ancient and the most revered scriptures, and the Eighteen *Silpas* or Arts, which included skills such as archery, hunting, and elephant lore, were taught, in addition to its law school, medical school, and school of military science. Students came to Taxila from far-off places such as Kashi, Kosala and Magadha, in spite of the long and arduous journey they had to undergo, on account of the excellence of the learned teachers there, all recognised as authorities on their respective subject

Taxila had great influence on Hindu culture and the Sanskrit language. It is perhaps best known for its association with Chanakya, also known as Kautilya, the strategist who guided Chandragupta Maurya and assisted in the founding of the Mauryan empire. Chanakya's Arthashastra (*The knowledge of Economics*) is said to have been composed in Taxila. The Ayurvedic healer Charaka also studied at

Taxila. He also started teaching at Taxila in the later period. Pāṇini, the grammarian who codified the rules that would define Classical Sanskrit, has also been part of the community at Taxila.

The institution is significant in Buddhist tradition since it is believed that the Mahāyāna branch of Buddhism took shape there. Jīvaka, the court physician of the Magadha emperor Bimbisara who once cured the Buddha, and the Buddhism-supporting ruler of Kosala, Prasenajit, are some important personalities mentioned in Pali texts who studied at Taxila

Aror is the ancestral town of the **Arora** Community. Aror is the medieval name of the city of **Rohri**, Sindh was once the capital of Sindh. Just as Aror is the ancestral home of Arora community, **Chhab** is the ancestral home of the **Chhabr** community. It is located in along the banks of Sindh river in the Jand Tehsil of Attock District in West Punjab. **Wahika** or Vahika is an ancient region located near Rawalpindi and home of the **Wahi** Katris. Its name in Sanskrit suggests a spring garden valley. The town of **Wah** is located between Hassan Adbal and Taxila. The natives of Wah were annihilated by the Epthalite or Abdali Pashtoon tribe and **Wahi** Khatris are their descendants. Another place related to the **Wahis** is **Takht-i-Bahi** (Throne of the water spring"), which is an archaeological site of an ancient Buddhist monastery in Mardan, NW Frontier. The site is considered among the most imposing relics of Buddhism in all of and has been "exceptionally well-preserved. **Madra** is the name of an ancient region and its inhabitants, located in the north-west division of the ancient Indian sub-continent. The Madra Kingdom's capital is located as the plains between rivers Ravi and Chenab in

The **Majha** region of West Punjab. Ancient epic, the Mahabharata that describes the armies of the Madra Kingdom led by King **Shalya**, marching from ancient Northwest Punjab to Haryana in support of the Pandavas. His sister Madri was the second queen of Pandu and mother of two Pandavs - Nakul and Sehdev. He however fought the battle on the the side of Kauravas against his own nephews.

Kekayas or Kaikeyas is the ancestral home of Khatri clan Kakkars. They were an ancient people attested to have been living in north-western Punjab—between Gandhara and the Beas River since remote antiquity. The Kingdom of Kekaya was founded by Kekaya who was the father of Kaikeyi, the step mother of Rama. Arora clan of Madan originate from the region. The Kekayas are said to have occupied the land now comprised by three districts of Jhelum, Shahpur and Gujerat in West Punjab. Ramayana lists the Kekaya metropolis as Rajagriha or Girivraja. which A. Cunningham has identified with Girjak in Khushab Tehsil on river Jhelum in the Jhelum district.

Sagala Sagala or Sangla is likely the city of Sakala mentioned in the Mahabharata, a Sanskrit epic of ancient India, later mentioned by Greek accounts as Sagala. The city may have been inhabited by the Saka, or Scythians, from Central Asia who had migrated into the Subcontinent. Dinga is ancestral home of Dhingra clan of Aroras. It is a city in District Gujrat, in West Punjab. Mong is the ancestral home of Arora clan Mongia. It is a small town in the Mandi Bahauddin District in West Punjab province of Pakistan.ween the rivers Jhelum and Chenab. Dinga is about 62 mi from the India-Pakistan border.

Reasons of Decline of IVC

Although historians agree that the civilization ceased abruptly, at least in Mohenjo-daro and Harappa there is disagreement on the possible causes for its end. Invaders from central and western Asia are considered by some historians to have been "destroyers" of Indus Valley civilization, but this view is open to reinterpretation. More plausible explanations are recurrent floods caused by tectonic earth movement, soil salinity, and desertification.

Decline theories include one that suggests that the slow East wards movement of the monsoons and increasing uncertainty was the eventual cause of the decline and demise. The civilization was formed in Baluchistan when it was much wetter than it is now, slowly the civilization travelled eastwards as the monsoons also moved eastwards and at some point in time the surplus agriculture, that formed the basis of the civilization turned into subsistence farming. With no surplus the cities lost their relevance, there was no surplus to be traded and precious stones to be imported etc. the whole economic structure fell apart. .

The civilization expanded over a large area as far as 1000 km away from the core Indus area, the required communications and skills which perhaps were not available and was beyond the capability of the ruling elite the outlying centers gradually started to ebb away. The newly added regions of Cholistan and Kathawair were attached the core civilization but as new centers in the northeast and southeast developed their own economic infrastructure their dependence on the central authority began to reduce. Their own regional affiliations and interests began to move them away from the central regime. The gradual silting up of the Hakra-Ghaggar River dented the economics of the civilization as people started to migrate

The decline was in my opinion, mainly caused because the civilization had stagnated. The similarity of: construction methods; weights; city planning; and architecture, which are touted as the strengths of the civilization, in fact suggest that for a long period of time the status quo was maintained.

I have a theory that there was internal strife and a significant and progressive part of the Indus elite migrated to the Sumer. The weakened leadership left behind was unable to come up with a response to the dwindling agriculture produce and in that failure the rationale for the cities to exist vanished. This level of sophistications was not achieved by the following Aryan civilization in the Ganga Jumna Valleys and in the Tamil South as well.

There is evidence of weak mechanism of violence. The weapons found at Mohenjodaro are weak as compared with the excellent tools. The spears are thin, without a rib; the spearhead would have crumpled up at the first good thrust. There are no swords at all. The sturdy knives and celts are tools, not weapons. The archer becomes an ideogram symbol, but there were no bronze arrowheads, only stone. Whatever authority controlled the people did so without much force. At one side of each of the cities there appears a "citadel" mound, fortified at Harappa in later times. Earlier it was simply an unfortified building complex on a 10-metre-high artificial platform, with ramps leading up the sides that would make ceremonial uses easy, but ruin defence. The lack of change on the Indus was not due to mere sloth or conservatism but too much deeper causes. It was a deliberate refusal to learn when innovation would have greatly improved matters. The merchants surely knew about canal irrigation in Babylon and Sumeria. No canals are discernible in any of the air photographs of the Indus region, apart from modern irrigation works. The simple open-cast bronze celt continued in use as a tool, though the axe and adze with a socket or a hole for the wooden shaft were certainly within the technical capacity of Indus craftsmen. The only specimens of the latter types are found in the top layers and belong unquestionably to invaders from the north-west whose graves (outside India) have such tools; so also with more efficient weapons such as swords, all foreign to the Indus culture

Of course, it is a puzzle why the Indus merchants did not adopt writing upon clay tablets from the Iraq counterparts with whom they traded. Why did they not take over the better foreign tools? Why not use canal irrigation and deep ploughing for agriculture? Some of them must have seen the heavy crops thus yielded on the Euphrates. The answer would be that the Indus merchant would not -profit from any of these improvements.

It follows that the land as a whole must have been the property of and directly administered by the great temple and its priesthood. Once established, they would insist in the way of most ancient priesthoods upon preventing all innovation. For them, change was not necessary; for the merchants change was not profitable

Kingship was not indispensable. The food surplus was yielded up by the primary producers without the use of much armed force. Religion, not prowess or violence, was the essential ideological force of the Indus society. This can be said repeatedly of Indian society at several later stages; the historical pattern was for peaceful religious stagnation to alternate with violent periods of war, invasion, conquest, or anarchy. On the Indus the stagnation was long and steady

The grain would be collected and distributed by the great temple. The granaries belonged to the citadel mound, being part of the complex or close, to it. The work of processing the grain was done by people who lived in adjacent quarters built to a uniform but rather mean pattern. These might have been temple slaves, of the sort known in Mesopotamia as qallu (gallu). To what extent the temple participated in the processes of manufacture is not known, but the participation must have been full, to judge by foreign parallels. It is notable, however, that the merchants seals do not show any female deity. The totem animals are male without exception. The very few human figures, where identifiable, seem also to be male. One possible implication is that the traders developed their own secondary cults in which the mother goddess had no direct share. This would then be true of the profits of the trade as well, in contrast to revenue from the land.

First, the rivers may have changed course, as happened so often. This would ruin the city as a port and make the maintenance of a food supply difficult. Secondly, the conquerors were not primarily agriculturists. They shattered the dams by which flood irrigation was made to deposit silt on a wider expanse of land. This signaled the end of cereal production, and so of the cities which had .already begun to decay from long stagnation. The really viable society had to grow again, as a combination of new and old.

The symptoms if decline were : sub division of houses; vandalized statues; un conventional burials ; collapse of several crafts ; end of sea trade ; decline in craftsmanship quality ;. These symptoms were possibly resulting from causes: vegetation changes; political strife by defacement of skeletons ; depopulation of the Hakra- Gakkar area. What really declined was: the political economy with its instruments of dominance; economic networks; and governance. There is evidence of varying narratives on the belief systems.

The IVC did not have temples or did not have an institutionalized system of worship. Vegetation changes, climatic changes also weakened the toes of the rural areas to the urban centers, the rural areas were no longer viable as these were not yet self sufficient. External trade was disrupted with the rise of Elam. There is also a possibility of strife within the priestly community, the merchants who travelled and had knowledge of technological changes, like irrigation; metals; other products, did not seek to bring these technologies to the civilization. The merchant class deemed that any technological change will strengthen the priestly class at their cost. The IVC stagnated and did not evolve and respond to changes in many factors because the elite were stymied by strife and self interest.

Aryans arrive

The Vedas composed in archaic, or Vedic, Sanskrit, generally dated between 1500 and 800 BCE, and transmitted orally, the Vedas comprise four major texts— the Rig-, the Sama-, the Yajur-, and the Atharvaveda. Of these, the Rigveda is believed to be the earliest. The texts consist of hymns, charms, spells, and ritual observations current among the Indo-European-speaking people known as Aryans. The early Vedic was the period of transition from nomadic pastoralism to settled village communities intermixing pastoral and agrarian economies. Cattle were initially the dominant commodity, as indicated by the use of the words *gotra* ("cowpen") to signify the endogamous kinship group and *gavishti* ("searching for cows") to denote war. A patriarchal extended family structure gave rise to the practice of *niyoga* (levirate), which permitted a widow to marry her husband's brother. A community of families constituted a *grama*. The term *vish* is generally interpreted to mean "clan." Clan assemblies appear to have been frequent in the early stages. Various categories of assemblies are mentioned, such as *vidatha*, *samiti*, and *sabha*, although the precise distinctions between these categories are not clear. The clan also gathered for the *yajna*, the Vedic sacrifice conducted by the priest, whose ritual actions ensured prosperity and imbued the chief with valor. The chief was primarily a war leader with responsibility for protecting the clan, for which function he received a *bali* ("tribute"). Punishment was exacted according to a principle resembling the wergild of ancient Germanic law, whereby the social rank of a wronged or slain man determined the compensation due him or his survivors

The Indo-European peoples (Aryans) had spread across northern India and had begun to live in settled villages and tribal states. These were ruled over by the leaders of prominent Aryan clans, now emerging as kings. It is probably around this time in ancient India's history that the four earliest castes appear in Aryan society: Brahmins (priests), Ksatriyas (warriors and rulers), Vaisya (the broad mass of tribesmen – farmers, craftsmen and merchants), and the descendents of conquered peoples relegated to a subservient role in society as Sudras (servants and labourers). This simple four-tiered caste system will become ever more elaborate as the history of India progresses. The **caste** system evolved after the Hindu religion achieved the Classical Hinduism status,

\

At this time also, a rich religious oral tradition is being developed, revolving around the doings of the Aryan's pantheon of gods and goddesses. This will later form the Vedas, the most ancient scriptures of the Hindu world and one of the most important foundations for Indian civilization

In the early twenties of this century extensive excavations done at Mohenjo-daro in Larkana district of Sind and Harappa in Montgomery district, both now in Pakistan unearthed some amazing revolutionary materials which tend to prove that in the pre-historic times, the people of Indus Valley had a high order of civilization.

Since these cities existed centuries before the advent of Aryans on this land, it suggests   that the language and culture of Punjab predate the Aryan culture At least five thousand years ago, the Indus Valley had a ' glorious civilization, not found in any other part of the civilized world It has been found that the lived in well-built brick houses with good floors, bathrooms, wells and rubbish pits.
The city had developed drainage system, there and its roads and streets were straight and wide. It can be said that its municipal life was much advanced and sanitation systems were thoroughly organized. A great public bath, 180 feet by 108 feet, with a large swimming pool, surrounded by galleries was a spectacular find of the whole excavations.

The people were well advanced in agriculture, tended sheep and cattle .and used vehicles for transport. 'Cotton cloth was in use which they spun and wove and their craftsmanship was of a high order. The discovery of photographic script reveals that they had an advanced art of writing. So far as religion was concerned the people worshipped trees, phallic stones, the mother goddess and also a male god.

Many historians are of the opinion that this civilization had a close 'affinity with the Sumerian civilization of Mesopotamia. Some seals of the Indus Valley found in Mesopotamia, established beyond doubt that an inter-relationship of sorts must have existed between the Indus Valley and the other lands of Western Asia, long before the recorded history of the world' Further it is also established that this great civilization owed little to the outside world and is no ground to believe that it was formed by immigrants from other countries. The cities of Harappa and

Mohenjo-daro were built by the people who had been living in the Indus Valley for several centuries before the Aryans entered India. This would suggest that:

1. The Aryans were not the first inhabitants of Punjab.
2. They did not form a well-educated and civilized nation. Their life style was of primitive nature and their occupations were limited to the raising of cattle, sheep etc'
3. The Aryan of that time had no perception of art and culture although they had their sacred scriptures like the Vedas with them and hence the Vedic language was also used in conversation.
4. The natives of this land had their own philosophy of life, religious quest and queries and -methods of meditation etc.
5. They had their own perceptions of art and culture.
6. They had their own art of writing which shows that they had a developed language and script.

The above facts clearly establish that the civilization of the Natives was much more advanced than that that of the Aryans who came to this land in groups as invaders' This is also an established fact that the Aryans borrowed much of what is known as the Aryan civilization from the Natives of Punjab.

1. They borrowed the concept of Karma and transmigration of soul from the original inhabitants of this region.
2. They borrowed their much adored deities like Shiva and Vishnu and some experts are of the opinion that even lord Krishna is a god of the pre-Aryan civilization- Goddesses like Durga, Kali and Chandi were also adopted by the Aryans from the inhabitants of the earlier civilization. The worship of trees and the belief in magic were also the contributions of the preceding civilization to the Aryan civilization.
3. The most popular Puranic stories about 'devas' and demons which cultivated the Aryan consciousness are also said to be the product of the influence of local civilization on the Aryan civilization.
4. So far as the dress was concerned, dhoti, the saree etc. were also adopted by the Aryans from the local people.

5. During ceremonies like marriages, the use of turmeric (haldi) and henna (mehandi) etc. was also acquired by the Aryans from the earlier civilization

6. The use of coconut, rice, beetal leaf nut (pan-supari) etc. in religious ceremonies was also due to the influence that the earlier civilizations had on the Aryans.

Significantly when the Aryans entered Punjab they were not a sophisticated people. They learned the art of a civilized living from the original residents of Punjab. There was possibly a two way exchange during which both religion and language evolved. Classical Hinduism and Sanskrit were born so to was classical Punjabi.

The Aryans did coexist with the locals, for the two ways exchange happened as there had coexistence for a long period of time, all this time there was low level strife and war .

The Aryans did not however, mix with the locals. Over a period of time the Aryans prevailed this resulted in the local population to disperse both to the north and south, those left behind were enslaved by the Aryans. After the Aryans themselves migrated to the Ganga Jumna valleys, they took with them some of the enslaved population and some were left behind, these therefore were the local or the non Aryan population who were left behind.

Now this whole discussion crystallizes into the following points:

1. The Civilization of Punjab is older than the civilization of the Aryan invaders.

2. The people of Punjab thus had a language and a script of their own.

3. The language of the Aryans that is the Vedic language was influenced by the Punjabi language of the time.

It is not necessary that the name of the language of that, time in Punjab: was Punjabi. But they had a script and a language which influenced the language and script of the Aryan who settled in these parts.

The region in that period possibly had a brief relationship with Iran, followed by longer periods of mixed Iranian Indian connection .This followed by the arrival of the Aryans and the prevailing culture of the Aryans is presented in the Rig Veda, which was possibly compiled by about 1000 BC. The book itself is religious in content with very little historical information. . Rig Veda does present some information about the Aryans. People.,.

The Vedic Aryans on arrival were a pastoral with nomadic habits The Gopas (cattle-keepers) were kept in high esteem. The rishi who composed hymns prayed to gods to bestow upon them many cows abounding in milk. The deities were invoked to protect the cows from harm, to increase the herds and to make pastures green. Cattle was the medium of exchange

The area which the Rig Veda culture encompasses is the Pakistani Punjab, , some small portions of the Doab of the Ganges and Jumna , it is likely that the culture encroached into parts of Afghanistan .This would approximately correspond to the area claimed by the Indus Valley Civilization

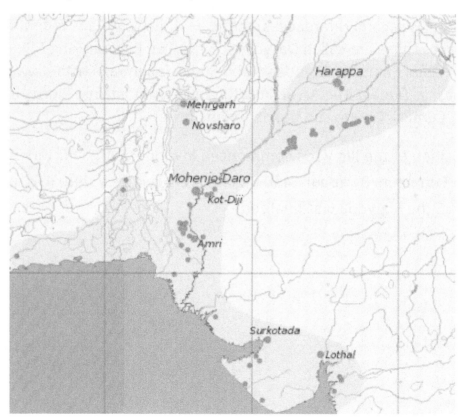

From the Rig Veda it would suggest that the Aryans saw themselves as culturally different from the locals and considered themselves superior to the locals (the later perhaps is unlikely to be correct as the locals were inheritors of a very sophisticate d civilization). They disliked the ways of the non Aryans, and applied derogatory epithets to them condemning their religious practices.

The Aryans brought in a language unrelated to any language of the sub continent, The Aryans spoke a Indo-European language whereas the non Aryans possibly spoke a Dravidian language or possibly a Munda language or possibly the mother Punjabi language.

In the oldest text of Hinduism, the Rig Veda, the warrior god Indra rides against his "impure enemies," or *dasa,* in a horse-drawn chariot, destroys their fortresses, or *pur,* and secures land and water for his people, the *arya,* or Arya. *Rig Veda* was passed down orally for some two thousand years before being written down .

The Rig Veda has several references to people whom te Aryans fought over cattle and pasturage. These are called Dasyus or Panis. The Rigveda king Divodasa fought Dasa Chief Sambara, Divodasas son Sudas fought against fellow Aryans as well as Dasas: as Dadas . Tne Aryan king Rjisvan fought against Pipru , other Dasas named are: Cumuri; Dhuni; and Varcin among others

The composition of the Rig Veda commenced in modern Afghanistan by a section of the Indo European. By about 1400 BC late IVC structures were in decline, by about 900 BC the Rig Veda was finalized.

Religious and Linguistics transformations

The Arya stay was a prolonged one some 1000 years long, during this stay there was a two exchange between the Aryan and non Aryan population , both religion and language evolved. Sanskrit evolved to Vedic Sanskrit to eventually evolve into classical Sanskrit, whereas Punjabi evolved to the post Vedic Punjabi. During this period the Punjab was culturally different from the rest of the sub continent. –

The closest relations to the Aryans at that point in time were the Iranians, whose language and sacred texts are preserved in various works known as Avesta, in inscription in Oil Persian, and in some other scattered documents. So great is the amount of material common to the Rig Vedic Aryans and the Iranians that the books of the two people show common geographic names as well as deities and ideas. The Aryans took into the sub continent names of streams whuch they had known before in Afghanistan and Iran

There is some discussion on who contribute to whom, but what is almost certain is that what are Called Hindus thought and Hinduism is not a simple growth from the pre Vedic religion to Vedic religion. There are elements other than the Vedic or Aryan which contributed to this development, since the Aryans interacted with the remnants f the Indus Valley Civilization it would be safe to assume that the other element that caused this change has to be the Harappan thought and religion.

Forests played a part in this transformation, but in the Rig Veda or in pre Upanisadic Vedas there is not mention of forests. . The authors of the Rig Vedas were residents of cities or villages and not of forests they were not people who retired to the forest to contemplate. The gods of the Vedas are not forest deities. They came in chariots drawn by horses. Non Vedic gods were associated with forests. Nearly all the Sivaite gods are non Aryan . Kali, Durga or Ayyappan .

Aryan religion is one where ritualism reins supreme. The offering of Soma at a sacrifice the most important feature of the religion, the Vedic text promotes this ritualism, the non Aryan element introduced an lack of stress associated with sacrifice and soma , , the concept of temples is introduced and the more abstract form of worship is promoted .

The Vedic religion is essentially the worship of a male deity, there are few goddesses and even these are of no great importance. The IVC source introduced the concept of goddesses as a creative power, thus we have Sri (goddess of wealth) and Bhumi (the earth) as the consort of Vishnu. Paravati as the consort of Shiva and Sarasvati as the consort of Brahama

The other significant element introduced by the non Aryan elements was animals, birds and trees, birds. The Vedic text does not refer to the animal or tree in any detail; it does however mention the horse which draws the chariot of the gods and the cow which provides milk. Birds and trees only come to mention in the Veda in a incidental manner not in a primal manner. After the impact of non Aryan elements the Vedic text does mention animals, cows achieve center place, various animals and birds are mentioned that carry gods. Thus Shiva has a bull, Vishnu has a kite, Brahama has swans. Vishnu rests on a coiled body of a serpent. Elephants, lion's tiger, buffalos etc. come into the picture as associated with deities. . Trees also became objects of worship. Banyan tree and other plants and creepers are associated with various powers. Thus the presence of the Divine was not restricted to temples but also all around in nature the Divine was present.

The other major element introduced by non Aryan sources was the concept of deification of man, great heroes, considered as gods, came down to earth as men for the protection of humanity. These were worshiped as gods in temples erected for them. There is no mention in the Vedas of gads coming to earth as human beings. In Post Vedic Hinduism God also appears in the form of animals.

There is Hunumat, the monkey god, there is Genesha, the man elephant god, Nandin, the attendant on Shiva , has the form of a bull. Skanda has the form of a serpent. The gods of he Vedas have no individuality and little concreteness', but later in Hinduism the divine form is more concrete

Indus Valley Civilization religion and Dalit religion

The identification of non Aryan elements that modified Vedic Hinduism, presented in the last chapter, can also be used to present the outlines of the religion of Indus Valley Civilization:

1. The importance of forests in the lives of people
2. Temple worship along with the contemplation of a more concrete form of the Divine
3. Elevation of animals, birds and trees to a higher level of place in the scheme of creation
4. The exaltation of the female form in the conception of the Divine
5. The creative aspect of the Divine
6. The divine appearing as a man amongst people.

The above outline of the Harrapan religion interestingly coincides with a loose characterization for the Dalit religion; this would suggest that the Dalits are the enslaved portion of the Indus Valley civilization population. Further it also establishes the linkage between the Indus Valley civilization with the Sumerian civilization The flood myth prevalent of Hindu epic literature is derived from the Sumerian flood myth.

Manu, in the mythology of India, is the first man, and the legendary author of an important Sanskrit law code.   Manu appears in the Vedas as the performer of the first sacrifice. He is also known as the first king, and most rulers of medieval India traced their genealogy back to him, either through his son (the solar line) or his daughter (the lunar line). In the story of the great flood, Manu combines the characteristics of the Hebrew Bible figures of Noah, who preserved life from extinction in a great flood, and Adam, the first man.

 The Shatapatha Brahmana recounts how he was warned by a fish, to which he had done a kindness, that a flood would destroy the whole of humanity. He therefore built a boat, as the fish advised. When the flood came, he tied this boat to the fish's horn and was safely steered to a resting place on a mountaintop. When the flood receded, Manu, the sole human survivor, performed a sacrifice, pouring oblations of butter and sour milk into the waters. a year later there was born from the waters a woman, who announced herself as "the daughter of Manu."

These two then became the ancestors of a new human race to replenish the earth. In the *Mahabharata* the fish is identified with the god Brahma, while in the Puranas it is Matsya, the fish incarnation of Lord Vishnu. The flood myth could well have been borrowed from the Indus Valley civilization sources. It true it would suggest that the Harappan people were fully aware of the Sumerian myths, Harappans and Sumerians were possibly related, sister tribes. These Sumerian myths, at least those which did not change over time, could well be myths form the primal sources and must therefore also prevalent I the Indus Civilization people.

The origins of untouchability can be traced back to the times when the Aryans invaded India around 1500 BC. They looked down upon the indigenous people as culturally and racially inferior. While some of the indigenous people escaped into the jungles, the rest of them were subdued and incorporated into the Aryan society as inferior castes. In the Later-Vedic period, the people who escaped into the jungles began to be called Chandalas. There was a lot of stigma against the Chandalas in the Later-Vedic period, but untouchability on a large scale appeared only between 600 BC and 200 AD.

Dalit writers have reacted bitterly to Hindu religious literature. Dalit writers have used those images and symbols in their literature that are appropriate for relating experiences. Dalit writers cannot forget that Hindu religious literature has nourished the unequal caste system. 'Rama, the killer of Shambuka, cannot be their ideal. Gita and Mahabharata, which support the caste system, cannot be honored. This is the perspective of Dalit writers. Dalit writers try to construct new myths instead of using the existing symbols and metaphors of Hindu sacred literature. When Dalit writers employ religious symbols, it was to deconstruct them, infusing them with new meaning and purpose.

The *Shudras or Dalits* have their own gods and goddesses even today, starting from that *Paraya* god *Shiva,* and his consort that *Parachi* – the *Jungli* goddess *Kali.* The gods of the *Shudras* have their own temples. What is more, even their goddesses have their own independent and exclusive temples - free from their consorts. These Temples have their own distinct but simple constructions, with bright colorful architecture, and with very little restrictions.

Shudras follow distinctly different but simple ritualistic practices of worship, that include offerings of meat, blood, and intoxicating home-made or community brewed liquor. Ceremonial occasions, invariably involve serving of food in public to the whole community. And the unique fact is that these Temples did not have any Priests. Anyone and everyone praying and or making offerings is at that time a Priest himself or herself. It is not that this is because the *Shadras* did not have the benefit of Brahmin priests.

The Problem of a caste Hindu Priest does not arise in the *traditional Shudras' Temples,* as there is generally no priestly-intervention or priest-intermediary between the praying *Shudra* and the god or goddess. Every *Shudra* can by himself or herself directly communicate with his or her god or goddess, casually in passing; or seriously with offerings and sacrifices, touching his or her god and or goddess personally and physically. But this does not mean that the *Shudras did* not or do not have any Priests. They always had and even now have their own Priests, who step-in on special occasions. But they were and still are uniquely different and distinct from those of other Religions and Communities. They were highly professional, great masters in their art and knowledge of rituals prayers and songs. The prayers and prayer songs etc were and still are in local languages, but chaste and pure, within the knowledge understanding and grasp of the common man of the community. These were professionals alright, but were not professional priests! They were and still are, ordinary members of the *Shudra Community,* attending to normal household and professional works like any other individual. But they were and are called, in only for formal ceremonies - such as those associated with death and organized marriages.

This again, even though a man and a woman, on their own choice secretively by themselves, or exclusively with only their close friends and confidents, without others knowledge can go to any of their own or chosen god or goddess for the occasion - anywhere in the Village, or on the roadside, or in the fields, or even in the jungles - to get married as per the custom they know or choose to adopt. This they may declare to the community, or may keep it as a secret till they choose to declare at a later date. That is perfectly valid, as for as the *Ati-Shudras* are concerned with-in their communities, whether there were any witnesses for the marriage or not or whether such a marriage proposal had the approval and sanction of the community, or was opposed by anyone else.

The cultural, economic and political ethos of the Dalitbahujan Goddesses(Pochamma, Kattamaisamma, Polimeramma, Yellamma, Mankalamma, Mareamma)/Gods is entirely different from Hindu hegemonic Gods and Goddesses (Lakshmi, Saraswati, Parvati, Durga). The Dalitbahujan Goddesses/Gods are culturally rooted in production, protection and procreation. They do not distinguish between one section of society and the other, one caste and the other.

In these stories there is no scope for creation of an enemy image. War and violence are not at all central to the philosophical notions of the people. Ritualism is a simple activity which does not involve economic waste. Despite there being such a strong sense of the sacred, Dalitbahujan society never allowed the emergence of a priestly class/caste that is alienated from production and alienates the Goddesses and Gods from the people. There is little or no distance between the Gods and Goddesses and the people. In fact the people hardly depend on these Goddesses/Gods. To whatever extent it exists, and contact is needed, the route between the deity and people is direct. Barriers like language, sloka or mantra are not erected.

The Hindu Gods are basically war heroes and mostly from wars conducted against Dalitbahujans in order to create a society where exploitation and inequality are part of the very structure that creates and maintains the caste system. The Hindus have a male-centered mythology and women are restricted to gender-specific roles and rendered sexual objects.

Though the brahminical Hindus claim that their tradition is rooted in non-violence, the truth is the other way round. All the Hindu Gods were propagators of violent wars. Their dharma is a caste dharma and their living styles, rich and exploitative. Production is made their first enemy. The fact that these Gods are approachable only through a priest and can understand only Sanskrit is enough indication that their alienation from the people is total.

The Dalitbahujans' Goddesses/Gods tradition is the exact opposite in every respect. These brahminical scholars and leaders who talk about Hindutva being the religion of all castes must realize that the Scheduled Castes, Other Backward Classes, and Scheduled Tribes of this country have nothing in common with the Hindus. For centuries, even when Dalitbahujans tried to unite all castes, the Brahmins, the Baniyas and the Kshatriyas opposed the effort.

Even today, no Brahmin adopts the names of Dalit Goddesses/Gods; even today, they do not understand that the Dalitbahujans have a much more humane and egalitarian tradition and culture than the Hindu tradition and culture. Even today, Dalit cultural tradition is being treated as meritless. If the Brahmins, the Baniyas, the Kshatriyas and the neo-Kshatriyas of this country want unity among diversity, they should join The Dalits and look to Dalitization, not Hinduization.

The trantric forms of worship, human sacrifice, walking on fire, are of Dravidian origin. According to the Smritis, the Untouchable is prohibited from hearing any Sanskrit scriptures, much less reading or writing them. Molten lead must be poured into his ears if he does - decreed Manu. Basham, the great historian, records, "It was with the conscious motive of preserving ritual and religious purity that all contact with the untouchables was avoided." That is why, the Dalits were not allowed into any temple in India for the last 3000 years. The reason was clear racial and religious distinctive.

The Vedic Aryans and the Dasyu slaves had distinct religions of their own. There was no chance of mixing the two faiths, at any time of history, because of the most stringent rules of untouchability and isolation. To put it more exactly, it was out of the greatest concern to keep the two faiths separate, that untouchability and isolation were stringently maintained. Therefore, to call a person as Hindu Scheduled Caste is absurd and irrelevant.

Siddharta, when under the pipal tree in Gaya became Buddha, he started profound upheavals in India with his new faith. Buddhism attracted many untouchables because it practiced no caste and no untouchability. The Buddhists rejected the authority of the Vedas and condemned blood sacrifice. The egalitarian outlook was viewed with great alarm by the Brahminical writings of the time - Yuga Purana, Mahabharata, Patanjali Bhasya, Bana, Manu and others. In spite of the Brahminic elimination of the Buddhism from India, the aspiration of the Scheduled Castes for an egalitarian faith did not end. The Neo Buddhist movement of today, when started from Nagpur in 1956 with Dr.Ambedkar and five lakhs of his followers becoming Buddhist must be understood in the light of this background. The quest continues equally into other egalitarian faiths like Kabir Panth, Nanak Panth, etc. Kabir made a great impact on the religious pursuit of the untouchables.

Kabir, while powerfully appealing to the untouchables, equally influenced Sur Das, Tulsi Das and Guru Nanak. The untouchables as a result joined the Kabir Panth and Nanak Panth in great numbers. Another significant impact of the monotheistic bhakti movement among the untouchables was initiated by Jagjivan Das of Lucknow, who was himself initiated by a Fakir. The movement, Satnami, as it was later called, euphorised monotheism with the abolition of all symbolism and castes, though later symbols and castes made partial re-entry. The above monotheistic pietistic egalitarian faiths in a personal God and brotherhood of classless believers are close to the Christian faith.

Thus the untouchable slaves in India, who are non-Aryan by race and religion have in the past 2500 years, voluntarily chosen several egalitarian faiths, that gave them religious and social satisfaction.

Worship of Pochamma: Pochamma is the most popularity of Munnuru*kapu* community Goddess in every village, there is a small Pochamma temple. The temple is a place where the deity exists, but not in order that regular *pujas* be conducted for her. Pochamma is not made the object of a daily Puja by the priest. Once every year the masses go to the temple with Bonalu (pots in which sweet rice is cooked) wash the small stone that represents the deity, and clean the temple and its surroundings.

 The people can approach the goddess without the mediation of a priest. They talk to the goddess as they talk among themselves. Between the people and Pochamma there is no priest.'Mother', they say 'we have seeded the fields, now you must ensure that the crop grows well one of our children is sick it is your bounden duty to cure here. If one listens to these prayers it becomes clear that there is a very human affair. There is nothing extraordinary about them. The people put small quantities of the 'bonam' food (which is known as padi) on a leaf in front of the deity. Finally, the chicken or sheep they have brought will be slaughtered. The dalit bahujans beat the dappulu (percussion instrument), while the young people dance and make merry.

Worship of Kattamaisamma: Katta Maisamma is a goddess of water, whose deity (a small stone) is kept on the bund of the village tank. She too does not require a big temple.people believe that Katta Maisamma is responsible for ensuring that the tank is filled. She regulates the water resources.

The farmers believe that right from the seeding stage to the cutting stage. She god protects the crop. The paddy fields below the tanks flourish because of her blessings.

Once in three years a major festival focusing on Kattmaisamma is celebrated. In some villages, several sheep, goats and chickens are killed and a big feast is organized. Rice is cooked and soaked in animal blood and sprinkled in the fields as *bali* (sacrifice). The belief here is that Katta maisamma must see to it that the fields yield good crops and that the crops become socially useful. As we say in our language, it must have barkati (prosperous utility).

Worship of Poleramma: Popularized among them is polimeramma (the border goddess). Polimeramma is supposed to guard the village from all the evils that come from outside to stop them at the boundary of the village. The duty that people assign to her is the protection of the whole village, irrespective of caste or class.There are several other village-specific, area-specific, caste-specific goddesses. Yellamma, Mankalamma, Maremma, Muthyalamma, Uppalamma, are some of them

Literature of the Vedic Period

The oldest literature of the Hindus is known as Vedas , which means knowledge. The essential parts of the Vedas consist of: hymns; prayers; spells; mixed with some prose. The Vedas are four in number: Rig Veda; Sama; Yagar; and Atharvan also known as Brahamana,

The **Brahmanas** are theological explanations; these were composed much later than the main text. The   Brahmanas include certain mystic trestises called the forest book.

 Upanisaids mostly are placed at the end of the Veda , the concluding part. This concluding part summarizes and crystallizes the essence of the Veda. The spirit of the Upansaid is opposition to rituals. Rituals are at time openly and other times obliquely condemned. The Upansiads uphold the primacy if Braham the creator and the main deity. The Upansiads distinguish between lower and higher knowledge, interestingly the Upansiads consider the four Vedas lower knowledge. These are philosophical books.

 Puranas are eighteen in number; these are popular sectarian compilation of mythology, philosophy, history, and the sacred law. . Much of the text comes from antiquity. Each of the Purana is roughly dedicated to the service of a particular godhead.

Mahabharta and Gita (which is a part of the former) are very highly regarded religious works, but these were composed after the time slice this investigation is interested in and are therefore not discussed further. Similarly Manu-Smrti is a leading work of sacred law but is also not discussed further as it falls in the time slice that we are not investigating.

Ramayana

Composed by Valmiki , it is devoted to celebration of the deeds' of Rama . The epic narrates a story that has been edited by Brahmans so as to transform the poem into a book of devotion consecrated to the service of God in the form of Vishnu. Rama, who is pictured as an incarnation of the deity has become the savior of mankind. Sita is revered as the model of womanhood. The epic has had a profound influence upon the Hindus It has set up ideals of manhood and womanhood.

The victory of good over evil is epitomized in the epic Ramayana (The Travels of Rama, or Ram in the preferred modern form), while another epic, Mahabharata (Great Battle of the Descendants of Bharata), spells out the concept of dharma and duty. the Ramayana recounts the kidnapping of Sita, Rama's wife, by Ravana, a demonic king of Lanka (Sri Lanka), her rescue by her husband (aided by his animal allies), and Rama's coronation, leading to a period of prosperity and justice. In the late twentieth century, these epics remain dear to the hearts of Hindus and are commonly read and enacted in many settings

The Epic comes with some issues, there are numerous versions of the Epic, secondly there are claims that the core story is derived from pre Aryans sources, some have even pointed out that the scene of the story is around Lahore and is in fact a story that war prevailing even before the Aryans arrived. Whatever be the merit of such assertions the fact remains that the Epic does contribute in a significant way towards the explanation of the faith, even if it is an older story the content of the Epic are nevertheless of great significance as they provide great contributions towards the explanation of Hinduism to the people.

The Epic presents a society wherein the four castes and four stages of life are firmly placed and explained: firm faith in the Vedas and the sayings of the seers is ingrained; sanctity of the cow and the Brahamana is emphasized; and the importance of religion and moral duties is explained.

The Epic also lays great stress upon education.The epic is considered a poetic creation based on mythology. , Sita is seen as the earth goddess and Rama an equivalent of Indra. The epic defines the ends which motivates human activities and every human being should strive to attain, these are; dharma (spiritual merit); artha(material advantage; and kama(gratification of desire). Dharma supersedes the other two, the epic presents the concept of drarma. The Ramayana presents a practical philosophy, underling ethics and religion. The higher philosophical truths are only touched incidentally. The epic is free from dogmatic and sectarian prejudice, which makes a special place for the epic in Hindu religious literature.

Ancient forgotten Mythology of the Punjab

My interest in the Indus Valley civilization has led me to the present languages of Pakistan (Punjabi, Sindhi and Seraiki) . Intuitively these three languages must contain some words and even structures from the ancient language of Harappa and Mohenjadaro .

There are also, semi related, two, other sets, of questions that I am seeking answers to.

1. There are words used in common usage , like Salada or Selada or Chellada (man with ability to appear and disappear), phopokutni (wise women in a negative sense) , Chawal (bad person), these seem to be a part of some ancient myths , but the myths and stories associated with these are not a part of the common Punjabi consciousness , in fact the first listed is only familiar to people of central Punjab. Are these related to some mythology and if so why have the myths not survived. Adding to this are words which have no apparent roots, like the word " kuri" a young girl , does not seem to have any linkages with either Sanskrit or Persian/Arabic sources.

2. There is this theory that the Chinese settled in North Punjab before immigrating to the Chinese Mainland. The tonal nature of the Chinese language and Punjabi suggest some linkages. Could there be linkages between Chinese or Munda myths and the above referred lost Punjabi myths. A Jat tribe of Punjab, Cheema , is linked to Chima or China and there are Munda linkages suggested with the origin of this tribe.

3. In the remote areas of Punjab and Sindh one hears strange sounds like : vivah (marriage) ; Sar (pond) , which are from the long forgotten Sanskrit .

I have a few questions related to some words of Punjabi language.

1. Salada (Chellada) is a word used in Central Punjab for a character that has ability to appear and disappear , a mythical character . Chaldea, from " master of deception " is a mischievous spirit , notorious for changing its form from and for teasing and diverting travelers , particularly at night

2. Phuphokutni is in common usage and is also a word used in Urdu
3. Chawal is also a word used in Punjabi

These words seems to be derived from myths,

The Dasyus worshipped demi-gods, demons, trees, animals, etc. The Chamars of northern India, to this day worship as gods, Saliya, Purbi, and as demons Vetal, Baital, Chural, Gayal, Paret, Pisach, Masau, Dund etc. The Untouchables of South Bihar have as their gods Surjahi, Barachi Vir, Basumit, Masana and Kunwar. Dr. Vidhyarti, the famous anthropologist studying the religion of untouchables, says they follow their own native festivals of Karam puja, Sohrai, Phagua Kadleta, Nawan, Jitaya, Chhat, etc. It must be noted that all these are etymologically Dravidi gods and Dravidi words.

 The above would suggest to me that the ancient lost mythology of the Punjab is linked to the Dalits and consequently to the Indus Valley civilization itself. It also links the Punjabi language to the Indus valley civilization.

The Indus Valley civilization had a tradition that the bride's sister hid the shoes of the groom and only gave this up after she received a "suitable" monetary contribution from the groom; this tradition is followed in marriages in Pakistan and Punjab even today.

The mythology or outline of that is presented above could only be related to the Indus Valley Civilization of to the Jatts who arrived in the Punjab after 1000 BC. This tradition is prevalent in Central Punjab the abode of the Jatts. These myths, however, do not find any similarity to the myths of the homeland of the Jatts, South Eastern Europe, although the Romanian stories and words do seem familiar to a Panjabi speaker. This would leave the IVC as the only source of these myths; these seem to be the long forgotten mythology of the Indus Valley Civilizations.

Economic History

Economic development during the time slice under consideration would begin with the decline of the Indus Valley Civilization. With early second millennium BCE persistent drought caused the population of the Indus Valley to scatter from large urban centers to villages. Around the same time, Indo-Aryan tribes moved into the Punjab from regions further northwest in several waves of migration. The resulting Vedic period was marked by the composition of the Vedas, large collections of hymns of these tribes whose postulated religious culture, through synthesis with the preexisting religious cultures of the subcontinent, gave rise to Hinduism. The caste system, which created a hierarchy of priests, warriors, and free peasants, but which excluded indigenous peoples by labeling their occupations impure, arose later during this period. Towards the end of the period, around 600 BCE, after the pastoral and nomadic Indo-Aryans spread from the Punjab into the Gangetic plain, large swaths of which they deforested to pave way for agriculture, a second urbanization took place

The Indus valley civilization was primarily centered in modern-day Pakistan, in the Indus river basin, and secondarily in the Ghaggar-Hakra river basin in eastern Pakistan and northwestern India. The Mature Indus civilization flourished from about 2600 to 1900 BCE, marking the beginning of urban civilization on the Indian subcontinent. The civilization included cities such as Harappa, Ganeriwala, and Mohenjo-daro in modern-day Pakistan, and Dholavira, Kalibangan, Rakhigarhi, and Lothal in modern-day India.

Inhabitants of the ancient Indus river valley, the Harappans, developed new techniques in metallurgy and handicraft (carneol products, seal carving), and produced copper, bronze, lead, and tin. The civilization is noted for its cities built of brick, roadside drainage system, and multi-storied houses and is thought to have had some kind of municipal organisation.

The Vedic period is named after the Indo-Aryan culture of north-west India, although other parts of India had a distinct cultural identity during this period. The Vedic culture is described in the texts of Vedas, still sacred to Hindus, which were orally composed in Vedic Sanskrit.

The Vedas are some of the oldest extant texts in India. The Vedic period, lasting from about 1500 to 500 BCE, contributed the foundations of several cultural aspects of the Indian subcontinent. In terms of culture, many regions of the Indian subcontinent transitioned from the Chalcolithic to the Iron Age in this period

A series of migrations by Indo-European-speaking semi nomads took place during the second millennium B.C. Known as Aryans, these preliterate pastoralists spoke an early form of Sanskrit, which has close philological similarities to other Indo-European languages, such as Avestan in Iran and ancient Greek and Latin. The term Aryan meant pure and implied the invaders' conscious attempts at retaining their tribal identity and roots while maintaining a social distance from earlier inhabitants.

By about 1500 BCE an important change began to occur in the northern half of the Indian subcontinent. The Indus civilization had declined by about 2000 BCE (or perhaps as late as 1750 BCE), and the stage was being set for a second and more lasting urbanization in the Ganges valley. The new areas of occupation were contiguous with and sometimes overlapping the core of the Harappan area. There was continuity of occupation in the Punjab and Gujarat, and a new thrust toward urbanization came from the migration of peoples from the Punjab into the Ganges valley.

Historians have analysed the Vedas to posit a Vedic culture in the Punjab region and the upper Gangetic Plain. Most historians also consider this period to have encompassed several waves of Indo-Aryan migration into the Indian subcontinent from the north-west. The peepal tree and cow were sanctified by the time of the Atharva Veda. Many of the concepts of Indian philosophy espoused later, like \ dharma, trace their roots to Vedic antecedents.

Early Vedic society is described in the Rigveda, the oldest Vedic text, believed to have been compiled during 2nd millennium BCE, in the northwestern region of the Indian subcontinent. At this time, Aryan society consisted of largely tribal and pastoral groups, distinct from the Harappan urbanization which had been abandoned. The early Indo-Aryan presence probably corresponds, in part, to the Ochre Coloured Pottery culture in archaeological contexts.

At the end of the Rigvedic period, the Aryan society began to expand from the northwestern region of the Indian subcontinent, into the western Ganges plain. It became increasingly agricultural and was socially organised around the hierarchy of the four *varnas*, or social classes. This social structure was characterised both by syncretising with the native cultures of northern India, but also eventually by the excluding of some indigenous peoples by labeling their occupations impure. During this period, many of the previous small tribal units and chiefdoms began to coalesce into Janapadas (monarchical, state-level polities).

The Iron Age in the Indian subcontinent from about 1200 BCE to the 6th century BCE is defined by the rise of Janapadas, which are realms, republics and kingdoms—notably the Iron Age Kingdoms of Kuru, Panchala, Kosala, Videha.

The structure of Indian society was characterized by caste. The distinguishing features of a caste society were endogamous kinship groups (*jatis*) arranged in a hierarchy of ritual ranking, based on notions of pollution and purity, with an intermeshing of service relationships and an adherence to geographic location. There was some coincidence between caste and access to economic resources. Although ritual hierarchy was unchanging, there appears to have been mobility within the framework. Migrations of peoples, both within the subcontinent and from outside, encouraged social mobility and change. The nucleus of the social structure was the family, with the pattern of kinship relations varying from region to region. In the more complex urban structure, occupational guilds occasionally took on *jati* functions, and there was a continual emergence of new social and professional groups.

Religion in early Indian history did not constitute a monolithic force. Even when the royalty attempted to encourage certain religions, the idea of a state religion was absent. In the main, there were three levels of religious expression. The most widespread was the worship of local cult deities vaguely associated with major deities, as seen in fertility cults, in the worship of mother goddesses

In addition to the archaeological legacy , there remains from this period the earliest literary record of Indian culture, the Vedas. Composed in archaic, or Vedic, Sanskrit, generally dated between 1500 and 800 BCE, and transmitted orally, the Vedas comprise four major texts—the Rig-, the Sama-, the Yajur-, and the Atharvaveda.

Of these, the Rigveda is believed to be the earliest. The texts consist of hymns, charms, spells, and ritual observations current among the Indo-European-speaking people known as Aryans , who presumably entered India from the Iranian regions.

Although archaeology has not yielded proof of the identity of the Aryans, the evolution and spread of their culture across the Indo-Gangetic Plain is generally undisputed. Modern knowledge of the early stages of this process rests on a body of sacred texts: the four Vedas (collections of hymns, prayers, and liturgy), the Brahmanas and the Upanishads (commentaries on Vedic rituals and philosophical treatises), and the Puranas (traditional mythic-historical works). The sanctity accorded to these texts and the manner of their preservation over several millennia--by an unbroken oral tradition--make them part of the living Hindu tradition.

These sacred texts offer guidance in piecing together Aryan beliefs and activities. The Aryans were a pantheistic people, following their tribal chieftain or raja, engaging in wars with each other or with other alien ethnic groups, and slowly becoming settled agriculturalists with consolidated territories and differentiated occupations. Their skills in using horse-drawn chariots and their knowledge of astronomy and mathematics gave them a military and technological advantage that led others to accept their social customs and religious beliefs. By around 1,000 B.C., Aryan culture had spread over most of India north of the Vindhya Range and in the process assimilated much from other cultures that preceded it.

The Aryans brought with them a new language, a new pantheon of anthropomorphic gods, a patrilineal and patriarchal family system, and a new social order, built on the religious and philosophical rationales of varnashramadharma . Although precise translation into English is difficult, the concept varnashramadharma , the bedrock of Indian traditional social organization, is built on three fundamental notions: varna (originally, "color," but later taken to mean social class--see Glossary), ashrama (stages of life such as youth, family life, detachment from the material world, and renunciation), and dharma (duty, righteousness, or sacred cosmic law).

The underlying belief is that present happiness and future salvation are contingent upon one's ethical or moral conduct; therefore, both society and individuals are expected to pursue a diverse but righteous path deemed appropriate for everyone based on one's birth, age, and station in life. The original three-tiered society--Brahman (priest), Kshatriya (warrior), and Vaishya (commoner)--eventually expanded into four in order to absorb the subjugated people--Shudra (servant)--or even five, when the outcaste peoples are considered.

The basic unit of Aryan society was the extended and patriarchal family. A cluster of related families constituted a village, while several villages formed a tribal unit. Child marriage, as practiced in later eras, was uncommon, but the partners' involvement in the selection of a mate and dowry and bride-price were customary. The birth of a son was welcome because he could later tend the herds, bring honor in battle, offer sacrifices to the gods, and inherit property and pass on the family name. Monogamy was widely accepted although polygamy was not unknown, and even polyandry is mentioned in later writings. Ritual suicide of widows was expected at a husband's death, and this might have been the beginning of the practice known as sati in later centuries, when the widow actually burnt herself on her husband's funeral pyre.

Permanent settlements and agriculture led to trade and other occupational differentiation. As lands along the Ganga were cleared, the river became a trade route, the numerous settlements on its banks acting as markets. Trade was restricted initially to local areas, and barter was an essential component of trade, cattle being the unit of value in large-scale transactions, which further limited the geographical reach of the trader. Custom was law, and kings and chief priests were the arbiters, perhaps advised by certain elders of the community. An Aryan raja, or king, was primarily a military leader, who took a share from the booty after successful cattle raids or battles. Although the rajas had managed to assert their authority, they scrupulously avoided conflicts with priests as a group, whose knowledge and austere religious life surpassed others in the community, and the rajas compromised their own interests with those of the priests.

From their original settlements in the Punjab region, the Aryans gradually began to penetrate eastward, clearing dense forests and establishing "tribal" settlements along the Ganga and Jamuna plains between 1500 and ca. 800 B.C. By around 500 B.C., most of northern India was inhabited and had been brought under cultivation, facilitating the increasing knowledge of the use of iron implements, including ox-drawn plows, and spurred by the growing population that provided voluntary and forced labor. As riverine and inland trade flourished, many towns along the Ganga became centers of trade, culture, and luxurious living. Increasing population and surplus production provided the bases for the emergence of independent states with fluid territorial boundaries over which disputes frequently arose.

The rudimentary administrative system headed by tribal chieftains was transformed by a number of regional republics or hereditary monarchies that devised ways to appropriate revenue and to conscript labor for expanding the areas of settlement and agriculture farther east and south, beyond the Narmada River. These emergent states collected revenue through officials, maintained armies, and built new cities and highways. By 600 B.C., sixteen such territorial powers--including the Magadha, Kosala, Kuru, and Gandhara--stretched across the North India plains from modern-day Afghanistan to Bangladesh. The right of a king to his throne, no matter how it was gained, was usually legitimized through elaborate sacrifice rituals and genealogies concocted by priests who ascribed to the king divine or superhuman origins.

Made in the USA
Monee, IL
20 January 2022

89501973R00037